Glass Town

Glass Town

Poems by

Lisa Russ Spaar

Red Hen Press

LOS ANGELES

Glass Town

Published by
Red Hen Press
P.O. Box 902582
Palmdale, California 93590-2582

Cover art: Detail from "Schoolroom of the Sky"
by Trisha Orr

Author photograph: Sydney Blair

Book and cover design by Mark E. Cull

Special thanks to George Garrett.

ISBN 1-888996-18-8
Library of Congress Catalog Card Number: 99-66649

First Edition

ACKNOWLEDGMENTS

Grateful acknowledgment is made to the following journals in which these poems first appeared or are forthcoming:

Poetry: "A Doubt"; *The Virginia Quarterly Review:* "Love Poem," "String Quartet," "February 29," "Writing *Jane Eyre,*" "Glass Town"; *Shenandoah:* "Hallowe'en" and "'I' Parson's Anne"; *Ploughshares:* "Rapunzel's Exile"; *The Kenyon Review:* "April"; *Quarterly West:* "First Night in the Tower" and "Rapunzel's Girlhood"; *Crazyhorse:* "Blind Boy on Skates"; *Verse:* "Rapunzel Shorn"; *The Hollins Critic:* "Something Important"; *The Sonora Review:* "Almost Too Serious," "Enough Luck," "By the Fire"; *The Pacific Review:* "Watching Lu Junne-nan Make the Poem 'Night Thoughts' by Li Po"; *The Atlanta Review:* "Rapunzel's Clock"; *Stone Country:* "Insomnia"; *Brilliant Corners:* "McCoy's Hands at the Piano"; *Pocket Poems,* ed. Paul Janezcko, Bradbury Press: "Piano."

Several of these poems first appeared in *Cellar* (Alderman Press, University of Virginia), a chapbook of 20 poems, and in *Blind Boy on Skates* (Trilobite Chapbooks of the University of North Texas Press), a chapbook of 8 poems. An Individual Artist's Award from the Virginia Commission for the Arts supported the making of this book.

Among the many gracious forces that helped shape this book, I must thank my family, Sydney Blair, Ōnē Buchanan, Stephen Cushman, Rita Dove, Kate Gale, George Garrett, Cynthia Lehmann, Susan Moss, Debra Nystrom, Dana Roeser, Mary Ann Samyn, Bob Schultz, Ellen Bryant Voigt, Charles Wright, my students, and, especially, Greg and Trisha Orr.

Contents

Scenes from Childhood
Kinderszenen after the piano cycle by Robert Schumann

The Separate Body

Rapunzel's Clock

The White Road

This book is for Pete,
and especially for
Jocelyn, Adam, and Suzannah:

"She looks as if she were thinking of something . . .
beyond her situation. . . . Her sight
seems turned in, gone down
into her heart."

—Charlotte Brontë
Jane Eyre

SCENES FROM CHILDHOOD

Kinderszenen

Scenes from Childhood

Kinderszenen after the piano cycle by Robert Schumann

> *It would have starved a Gnat—*
> *To live so small as I—*
> *And yet I was a living Child—*
>
> —Emily Dickinson

1. Foreign Lands, Foreign People
    Von Fremden Ländern und Menschen

I'd crack the heavy atlas' spine
to wings, its sewn pages flat
beneath my elbows, body sprawled
behind me, lost, abstracted

by the maps' allure, the bitten
shapes of continents, pink rings of atoll,
of isthmus, of peninsula named and cast
in the blue, gradated wash of ocean—

and all this someplace-else trapped
by a compass grid of longitude and latitude,
the world prostrate and reduced,
my own part of it a nectarine jigsaw

piece, a child's cut-out bird, caged
and one-dimensional despite the brave illusion
of meridian. I couldn't breathe.
No wonder Atlas strained

to shoulder up such planar,
celestial mathematics, and make room
enough below for the uncurling vertebrae
of ferns, the cypress' minarets

gilded in a trill of wind. And the trodden
courtyard, resounding with the race and cries,
where breathless Atalanta pauses still
to pick three golden apples up,

then rises, the wash of her body's defeat
redeeming the pink dust.

2. A Curious Story
   Kuriose Geschichte

        for LE and SG

By day, the abandoned carousel
tilts in sunshafts, a broken cookie,
a ditched cartwheel. She moves
among the impaled horses,

holds her empty hand out flat
to the glazed *rigor mortis*
of their lost happiness. In her backpack,
an ice pick and a poisoned apple

wrapped in a napkin. Along the field
behind the hulled midway and the tattered awnings
of concession stands, ripe plums thud,
engorged, purple thumbs

imprinting the ground. She smells them,
and the soldiers camped and smoking
by the far woods' edge.
At night she sleeps in weeds

beneath the upright O of the ferris wheel.
The dwarf rocking in the top seat,
near the stars' clots, throws down
old seeds popped to snow. The tacky ones

near the bottom of his paper sack
come down in twos and threes,
and she opens her mouth, parts her legs
to show him her tattoo shaped

like the p-ipa of the ancient Yüan dramas.
Around it, a thicket of thorns.
Under the black moon, she touches the strings,
her fingernails long and blue:

the dwarf laughs,
and she laughs, a music spiry and crooked
as the hurdy gurdy's hobbled chuckle,
briery map that lights her way.

3. Playing Tag
    Haschemann

Across the lawn's glossary
of shadows they are still chasing
one another. No sound but the glottal
music of exertion, small shrieks of escape,
or capture. Such a tempest, such a stillness
as dark falls: the pitiless syntax
of children's games among the sculptural
boxwood and bowed forsythia.
Among the magnolia's slick tongues,
beneath its cool, agnostic stars,
some are hiding; some stand still, unfurled
as candles. Others open, blossoms, heady
cups of scent—and these, these are bruising,
splaying, then they're falling:
they were playing, now it's over, now they're *it.*

4. Child Asking for Something
   Bittendes Kind

But what? Her parents' shelves
are full with plenty, towels
folded and stacked like loaves,
snug cans filed in the cupboards,
crackers poised in paper sleeves.
Erect and flush, closed books
fill their cases; and a sleeping arsenal
of sorted cutlery she glides in
and out on a drawer's casters,
just to see her face held a moment
in the knives' dull blades.
Still, she seeks out empty spaces,
though there aren't many: the dusty
locker beneath the bed's low-slung springs;
a curtained nave the skirt of her mother's vanity
table makes around her; and, most often,
the closet where she crouches,
heels-down into a cobbled pile of shoes,
the hems of the grown-ups' coats and jackets
just brushing the roots of her bangs.
Through a slit of light she spies them
as they move about their room, tumbling
a heavy wristwatch onto the dresser,
folding shirts on the bedspread.
She holds the place their legs would be,
if they could be still and quiet;
if they could stand even a minute
in the invisible darkness, with nothing
to do but watch her bright and hungry motion
across the lighted span.

5. Enough Luck
   Glückes genug

With sticks, we switched the blowze
of suburban pollen, Chinese-restaurant kitsch
mimosa and grill smoke adrift
over stockade fencing.
In the one remaining field out back
a creek ran sweet with dog skulls
and minnows and sudsy run-off
from the new houses going up,
the catacomb foundations
of open, flooded basements agape
on construction lots scraped raw
and piled with sour lumber.
Still, the nests we built there
of broken straw and old Christmas trees
made this garden secret.
Fresh mounds marked our losses—
goldfish buried in Band-Aid boxes,
the hieroglyphic stars of cigarette butts,
and moldy magazines, swollen
to small accordians that we fingered,
lingering over what we saw
in the spotted cartographies
of rain and rotting.
Once we even fell asleep
to the utterance of sun and indian grass—
the felicitous doze of orphans,
of monks—and woke to Joey Barbett
standing over us, practicing
with his father's bow and arrow,
before he turned and ran away.

6. Something Important
   Wichtige Begebenheit

At the end of a day watching younger
siblings play in the ocean,
I ventured down to the shore
with a child's bucket.

Enough of the warm sea I carried home
to glaze the pail's cargo of shells,
so glistery under water,
dull as toenails in the air.

In our room that night,
sisters asleep around me,
I put the bucket's sloshing,
plastic rim to my teeth,

filled my mouth with salt,
held tight my lips, a pursed omega,
dribbling as I crawled
to the place outside my parents' bedroom.

Mouth to the metallic slit below the doorknob,
I blew it all through the minuscule
rooms and ratchets of the keyhole:
such a sight from the other side,

filaments of spray alighting on the shag,
harmless as any wedding night razzing—had anyone been watching.
But this is all a lie. In our modern tract house
there were no keyholes, no privacy,

no ceremony. One of my mouths was newly red,
and all knew it. And so now I could not swim,
must sit apart. The bucket's water
my father emptied out beside the carport;

the shells my family used
as ashtrays, or dumped into a shoebox—
twisty, empty houses shucked
and sold by the sea that was once their everything.

7. Dreaming
  Träumerei

> *No one should consider anything his own,*
> *except, perhaps, a lie—*
>
> > —St. Augustine,
> > *The Confessions*

To lie is to be awake, to fly,
to spy from the ceiling the Witch
chiding the secret center of the house,
web of shifting halls, and rooms
with window ledges to leap through
into an escapade of leaves
and tree trunks rough as the legs of fathers,
giants let out to tame the Antic night,
its crowded attic lit by mild, suicidal stars.
To follow. To raise the sea with a willow switch,
and ride waves wrapped
in black lace, spine curving,
legs re-turning to water, water
to salt, to air, to cloud—ink on ink—
a glide—but by then its rolling pane
of glass goes gray, winking, heavy-lidded,
and all the world is breathing again,
sour bedding and nostrils
stirring to the slapped flank,
the old song of let-down, that slow,
mammalian motion, its extinguishing
notion that to waken, after all, is the lie.

8. By the Fire
   Am Kamin

Tsk, tsk of the metronome—
and the fire her mother laid earlier
pelts dully against the closed glass
of the hearth.
The nocturne is a glass house
the girl is building against her will,
in impossible chain reactions of marked
stave and struck key resounding
from the hidden felts and sinews
of the black piano, cavity she's afraid
to lift the lid of, and look inside,
theatre of her shapeless longing.
Tonight, the turrets teeter up, spiral
crystals of stair and transparent landing.
There's a window there, at the top,
white sheets lifted to the ceiling.
Lovely, her mother remarks, passing through
the room. From the dizzy air,
the girl feels more than sees
the woman behind her wrench the glass
doors open, poke at the charred,
stigmatic limbs of wood,
the ravelly thud and crack of fire
leaping again from the dark, ash-silted cave.

9. Hobby Horse Rider
   Ritter vom Steckenpferd

Why not straddle
my own vestigial tail,
and scribble every story
of the house with its blunt
end, cold clomp
of the cellar stairs,
plush tread of carpet, scrip-
scraping across kitchen
tiles, then a hurtling
on the raft
of my own bed, where waves
roil around me
like the millennium push
of glacier, of pressed ore,
of time I'm jumping,
I'm rocking through
on the stripped backbone
of a beast whose all-
head and frozen eyes
spur me to be
not just mind, and mind-
ful, but all I am,
but wild, but animal.

10. Almost Too Serious
  Fast zu ernst

Guess, she said with her body's
digression, her new schooling
in refusal. Hawking
her clues, she left pools
of spittle behind the pews
at church, in tissues,
on the school linoleum.
She gave it all away
repeatedly, deliberately—
hair, welts of breasts, skin
thin as petals—
and her ribs' small hive hung
empty, begging the question
that swarmed like a laugh-track
above the held breath of her life.

11. Scaring Someone
   Fürchtenmachen

The fathers are lions,
haloed by gin, leaping out
from the privet hedge soaked
with new dark and the day's
sprinkler-dose of water.
In shirtsleeves white
as streetlamps,
they stalk the *arbor vitae*,
the slatted picnic benches,
their growling a tenor
to our low, electric,
swallowed thrill of terror.
Dull, their watches glow
with the weightless heft
of fallen stars, and still
we hide from them, delaying
the inevitable *frisson*
of capitulation, of flicked-on
lights and screaming, the mothers
appearing, the party ending,
the mock dragging off
at last to the curb,
where the cars of departure
crouch—empty, waiting.

12. Child Falling Asleep
Kind im Einschlummern

The corner of the room
is wordless as a lap
but less impatient.
There she must sit, lower lip
wet with a dribble of spit
that threads down ever
so slowly, spotting
the paper sign she wears
like a bib around her neck—
I AM A BAD GIRL.
The letters are blocked out
like the ribs between the panes
of light that filter through
the drawn curtain.
Blue boats rock there,
sheeted against the late
afternoon's parade of child-
shriek and street and sun.
She tries as hard all day
as her mother tries to be good,
but who can blame them—the mother,
tired as she always is, for falling
asleep on the couch after lunch,
or the little girl for taking up
a stick, and following the noon
sidewalk's bald sheen down
to the forbidden river road,
where gaudy cars rocket past
and, between them, in green, brushy
glimpses, she can see the water winking?
Cross over, it seems to be singing
to her now, *You will never know arms
as guiltless as mine.*

13. The Poet Speaks
  Der Dichter spricht

The sharp surprise of air
after so much soaking in of the dark—
and my own, unused ribcage wheezing up
and down, newly practicing
against the Arctic expanse of sheet,
a floe of window-light, white rifts
of crib-bones rising. My mewing
in the winter of the empty room,
my stillness in the gasp
of their amazement: large, planetary
faces passing over, coming closer,
garbling down into the place
where I lie, pinned by the fruited
weight, the loaded hold of my head.
Spastic, my limbs bat over me,
pelting my own face, entering
my mouth. Everything's
inside me, what I know of the miraculous,
stellar sponge of cerebral matter,
the circuitous paths of becoming,
of milk's sweet way.
Have you wondered whether God
has legs to walk into our rooms,
arms to lift us when we cannot rise?
And whether, once words finally come
to us, their clumsy edges cast
indelible shadows on the light?
What truths I would tell you,
if only I could—

The Separate Body

Moon Travellers
with Report

1.

A girl balances her body
in the half-melon of a moon,
rocking, rowing her craft
across the starry haze
of a sheet of mimeographed paper.
In the margin, my daughter shows me
the characters for "two-end
moon-boat," phrases from a poem she's learned
visiting her friend's Chinese class:
only she was light and green
enough to sail the heavy orb
of tears above the sea

2.

A box of sleeping chopsticks,
the speckled scoop of a skin-thin
teacup, this bin of packaged explosives,
put away for winter,
whose ornate tissue wrappings are alive
with names: "Sky Garden—36 Shots,"
"Dragon Dancing With Phoenix,"
"Yellow Bees"—"Moon Travellers
                    with Report"—
immigrants with uncoded messages
from the world she craves.

3.

Dutifully, joyfully,
she studies the characters, marking
their sickles, their hooks
and arbors in the paper grid of quadrants.
Here are the pictures for *up*
and *down*. In class, two big Chinese boys
laughed at her American accent, her writing,
but here, at home, she stirs black sticks
of ink into a stone well of water,
fills her brush, the rice paper thick, suddenly,
with the tongues her leaves make, practicing.

4.

She plays with Joy, the adopted Chinese daughter
of American friends. A baby, Joy
needs no translation. **She throws**
the doggy down, I pick it up.
She throws it down, I hand it back.
We do this all afternoon, laughing.

5.

Orphanages full of girls.
Girls full of orphanages.

6.

This she does know, the story
of the moon princess: "She was good
but the Emperor was bad.

Again and again he mistreated her
until one night she tried to kill him
as he slept. Sly he was, one eye
always open, and he seized her—Death,
he decreed, would complete her sentence.
But the gods were grateful
for her goodness, and spared her.
Seven guards escorted her into heaven.
Look up, you can still see
her sad white face, there, trapped among veils."

7.

"This," her teacher commends,
bending over her, "is what we strive
for, an effortless obedience, a wild
order, what we call—," and, here, pointing
to my daughter's paper where she has painted
a leaping horse, its tail a buoyant skein
of stroke and light—*flying white.*"

8.

Some girls were lifted from the ground
into huts, held there,
"twixt heaven and earth"—
belonging to neither—
until the moon's eye closed
and opened once again.
In seclusion she must drink only
through the straw of swan's bone,
hollow flute, divested
of the straps of muscle made for flight.

The girl dreams of this creature—
ugly duckling, mysterious geisha
of the culverts, the park ponds;
all night, she tugs at a heart-beat's pulse
through the bridges' arches and shadows,
a wake of wings adrift behind her
on the silver water.

9.

Long, spindrift trails
of chrysanthemum fireworks fall from there
to here, from milky, smoke-scarred night
to our snow-crusted yard, so ghostly
and pocked with shadows
it could be the moon,
as though these acrid blooms
could heal the old rifts—
heaven and earth, girl
and dream . . .

10.

How the Chinese character for **middle**,
for **between**,
makes a pierced heart.

Recital

In the teacher's kitchen, we fidgeted
and were told to hush among the gladioli
presiding over trays of tri-tiered sandwiches

and the punchbowl of sherbet ice floes
swimming in ginger ale for afterwards.
If only it *were* afterwards,

and not the agony of **before**,
the memorized staves crisscrossing
our brains like fences gored

with all the notes that could—
and probably would—go wrong.
I blame those first recitals

for setting up a sham of perfection
beyond the limits of my body
and my ability: the mortification

of hurtling through what should instead be
music—flawed and surprising—
before an audience of shamefully

smiling instigators, as fearful as we,
suddenly, that their lives would be exposed
in one misstruck key, or two, or three . . .

Blind Boy on Skates

In the air: smoke, voices of the others,
coughing of trucks in the cornfield he came through
with his sister's skates and extra socks
for padding the empty toes.

A deep mass of shadow on thin blades,
he's not allowed to be here,
on skates, on the creek become a road,
miraculously accepting his weight—
creek into which arms had let him down
once in summer, screaming, his limbs
breaking the surface, and cold,
the *blue* taking his legs away—

He's balanced, safe, but knows that movement
is the only way to remain upright—
he thinks about going forward,
about that risk. For him, it's like
the sentences he types at school:
"You asked about the blue was, well, for me
the place the tractor makes in snow,
my head the same, my pillow in the morning"—
He can't say yet, to the teacher:
but I *can't* go back to see what I've said
to make it work together—
what's behind is past,
unravelled, lost.

He cannot say, life for me
is temporal, not a bottle with a thin neck
and a glass for receiving,
not a jar with a waist through which moments
accelerate and then deposit in a reservoir.
Motion is my only chance to be.
What I am is the thread of pulse under wool,
the slight twist of my ankles.
What I have is the clean,
blue clip of my own running steps,
and the screaming behind me,
and the truth I put my arms out
before me to receive.

Valentine's Day

Our world was arrested:
even secrets hung between us
in frozen trails. The neighborhood

lay shelved beneath a glacial
glaze, edges bitten where the small
sun smeared its cold lava

down white-packed streets.
The anomie of no school for weeks.
And all the low-slung seats of swings

were swallowed, lost in drifts,
their frozen chains rising like stripped stalks.
Our fathers' carports tilted, drowning

in snow. Everywhere, a new kingdom—
even the back field's bayberry thickets
succumbed, contorted in postures

of lace and wreckage. Opaque windows stared
from the backs of far-off houses.
And at last the blushless nicotine

breath of a boy whose tongue slid
against mine, whose cold thumbs
and fingers tugged my little breasts,

miraculous under such layers.
Later, urine tunnelled into my seat of snow
as I crouched under the sky's remote,

electric display—could any Grace
really come from there? In mimicry,
bonfires burned in drums behind us

at the pond's edge, where the scrapes
and cries of younger children at play rose
above transfigured water. Then, the closer

grunt of his boots.
But even the steam of his piss
brought no breath of any other season

than this one: all the remnant
wild animals bent and waiting
in the stricken woods.

Girl Scouts

Heads bent to task in the school
gymnasium, we sewed badges
to green sashes, our little awards—
emblems of the Pot and Needle,
the Library book, and the Key—
and of Camping, which in New Jersey
meant mosquito-bitten huddlings
on damp sit-upons around a smoking grill,
the highway whining faintly
through the sassafras groves
and Trees of Paradise.
Once I awoke with my face
pushed out under the mildewed hem
of a tent into raw, earliest morning,
my sleeping-bagged body trapped
back on the inside in the greenish dark
of other girls. Once, after a meeting
at her house, my leader's older daughter,
a senior scout, invited me to her room.
There she perched on the buttercup
wedding cake of a canopied bed,
a beauty mark caught in the adult down
of her upper lip, and showed me
the martial cross of two full sashes
of accomplishments strung across her breasts.
On her bedside table lay a corsage,
its bud shriveled to a brown beak
still pinned to netting, and behind,
on the wall, two shelves of plastic dolls
from different lands, identical faces
with different-colored hair and skin,
their molded plastic limbs held in place
by twisted rubber bands
noosed and strung across the cavities
where their hearts might have been,
if they were real—

I encountered her again, a couple years later,
on a chance, moonlit walk to the latrine
at Camp Sakajewea; several troops
were winter camping in cabins,
and there was snow, so we could clearly see
the silver fox, eyes blue as ice,
on the path where a light wind
leafed through her ruff of neck fur.
She stopped us with her stare
and held us there, a phantom watching,
until she turned, dropped scats, and loped
into the woods behind the wooden toilet.
We stood awhile, the older girl and I,
then eventually climbed up
and took our turns inside.
Which one of them was I thinking of
and why didn't I hurry more,
as I bared my back side to that well,
its draught edged with the threat
of another world, and with the dark perfume—
hung like my own frozen panting
in the stall—of the accumulated waste
of years and years of girls?

Hallowe'en

On the night of skulled gourds,
of small, masked demons
begging at the door,
a man cradles his eldest daughter
in the family room. She's fourteen,
she's dying because she will not eat
anymore. The doorbell keeps ringing;
his wife gives the sweets away.
He rubs the scalp
through his girl's thin hair.
She sleeps. He does not know
what to do.
When the carved pumpkin
gutters in the windowglass,
his little son races through the room,
his black suit printed with bones
that glow in the dark.
His pillowsack bulges with candy,
and he yelps with joy.
The father wishes he were young.
He's afraid of the dream
she's burning back to,
his dream of her before her birth,
so pure, so perfect,
with no body to impede her light.

Anorexia

I loathe the blade
that enters a body
in order that what is slaughtered
might be eaten,

but love the blade
held next to warm flesh,
reflecting what is still alive,

and carry the sharp edge close,
a cold locket
between my breasts,
a thin mirror
whittling away
at what remains over the bone—

but slowly,
so it might never be said, later,
that anything but love
ever existed between these two:
the blade, and the body.

Watching Lu Junne-nan Make the Poem "Night Thoughts" by Li Po

Hair's-breadth markings, garden trellises,
Box-like rows of espaliered trees
To support the reader's weight.
Just louder than the thin, musical scraping of the pencil,
He spoke for me in English of the lonely man
A bright moon wakens; but it was in Chinese—
In his one-syllabled utterances that echoed the pencil's tracing,
And in the crooked, ancient pictures
Arranged, despite all wildness, into orchard rows—
That I understood the man who watched the frost on his floor
Dissolve to moonlight as he fully wakened
Far from home, and how, for the watcher with no one to speak with
Just then, there is a sad, shared joke in the world's old language
Of desire, the eye's tricks, and the separate body.

Rapunzel's Clock

Rapunzel's Girlhood

In the house where I lived
before the tower,
we kept a tub filled with carp,
sleek secrets cruising the black water,
orange as embers.
Their mouths were round as my wrist
and always pulsing for more
of the grain we fed them.
I have a mouth with no tongue
and I explored it in my room
as far as my fingers could reach.
For some reason, I'd close my eyes
when I did this,
and always I'd picture those fish,
circling stories below in their basin,
sometimes coming to the surface
where I'd glimpse their large, wild eyes,
the fret of their flesh, elusive
as answers bobbing into view
in my Magic-8 Ball toy—
"Fat Chance" or "No Way"
and sometimes "It's in the Bag."
My lonely body asked my questions
for me—the dull ache of bones growing
overnight, of eggs preerupting inside me,
thimble breasts hot as coals—
and always the crone's hands filling
my bath, shearing my dress up,
testing the steam. It took two hands
for her to wrest a terrified fish,
pin it beneath her sodden knee,
slit its throat. I was always surprised
that something so hidden
could be exposed that way, the guts
coiled and glazed with musk,

little ladders of bones I'd prop
against my sill for the mice to climb—
and the meat I'd close my mouth around,
my tongue pressing all the remnants
of ocean echo down my throat
before I'd spit the tough flesh out.

Rapunzel's Exile

I was told to lie down in the cart, and I did. My braided hair mixed with straw under me to catch the blood I seeped. Then she covered me with heavy furs and brush. The night was stark and cold, the stars close and multiplying like cells as we creaked along under them a long time. We crossed creeks, water hissing up through shelves of ice. She pulled the whole time. She was a strong woman.

When I'd first felt the blood darken my skirt in the garden, I knew she'd cursed me for my new game, tossing stones over the wall, and someone—who?—tossing them back. All that day, she paced while I lay in her bed, waiting to die. All that night we travelled.

At dawn we were deep in a forest, so tangled we had to ditch the cart and pick by foot through roots and brambles. Ravines pitched and rose. We waded thigh deep in leaves and water. I watched her tough haunches, the rope around her waist that tethered my neck. The sky grew heavy with pent snow, and still we walked in woods so old and dark at noon the owls cried. The one who'd held my face, called it her "sun," had turned to me her wordless back. Behind her, I had no choice but follow, twelve years old, bent and sopping wet with shame and terror. Even when we came, finally, to the cleared place where the tower rose dully in weak moonlight, and I gasped "God-mother!," she would not turn to look at me. Her knife flashed quick to cut the rope, then pointed through the low door. I cried "no, no"—I pleaded and grasped for her—but the bright blade held me back. On my knees inside, I groped the stairs. The cellar draft above me fell upon my face, and I knew that this place had been made ready for me all the years that she had loved me. And I guessed that this was love, too—not the see-saw play of stones lopped over a garden wall, but my lonely climb upward, and the thick scrape of mortar over shoved and piled stones, behind.

First Night in the Tower

At the bed's four corners,
torches strapped with oily rags
flared to scare off bats
sucking strung-up apples in the eaves.
She lay awake under piled skins
listening to the hiss
of snow on coals
in a vented grate,
and to the velvet scissor snap
of wings.
Everything was touched
by the brazier's red,
the way we imagine the womb to be—
cast in a little candlelight, a warm
Italian restaurant—instead of blackness.
They say we're born twice.
Near dawn, she rose and pushed aside
the window's thick drape.
Below, miles of new, effacing snow,
as if her being there had no history.

The Hunters

She rarely saw them from the tower,
even in winter, but could hear them,
hounds tearing holes in the air,
the raucous taunts of crows,
blown horns erupting.

The hunters' hunger mocked
the ecstatic thonking of the geese,
whose strong whoosh and soughing
wingbeats filled her quiet days.
As a child, she'd thrown herself down

to wait for them, spine pressed flat
to the stones of the Crone's paths—
first a faint racket beyond the wall,
and then they'd be over her,
the late sun gilding their hieroglyph,

blocking out her sky, and she'd feel them
beating inside her—but not the way
the old woman's heart hammered her ribcage,
pressed against her body at night.
This new clamor lifted her.

From the tower, she once saw
an arrow-stuck grouse shudder in air,
then drop. She knew the heft of its body
falling into the uplifted arms
of birch and sycamore.

On winter nights before her banishment,
she and the Crone sat in the cellar
with wet laps, the boiling kettle
bobbing with carcasses, their fingers picking fur
and feathers off of rabbits, hens.

Even that far down in the ground,
she'd hear the geese passing over,
distorting her heart.
And when, later, she'd draw
her hand's blade across the cooled pot's

mealy plate of down and fur scud,
and clear a space, she did not see
her own heartface, pale and smudged
with blood, but their swift, sure arrow
moving across the red water.

Rapunzel at 14

I've watched this before, the winey rust,
the haze accumulating in woods spread below me.
It's as though I were a god,
spying on the world from the air—
except that in the tower's cellar-cool room
at my back, the chamber pot is full of blood
and flies.
                              What's happening
to my eyes, that I can see now
with hawk's clarity the smallest mouse
tunneling through field straw, feel the red river
of fox moving toward the thicket
of last grapes?

I hold my mouth open, teeth bared
to the wind. Vegetables rot

in my keeper's basket, as birds
wheel and hurtle through the tower,
liming the flags and sill.

The green world's absent, a terrible nostalgia.
Still, so **what** that the world is dying?
Nothing's ever fallen past my shoulders
that wasn't part of me.

Rapunzel's Fall

At night, falsetto,
he'll mimic the Crone.
Believing it's her,
she's tempted not to answer.
Finally, her candle licking
the window's black hole,
the uncoiling snake of braid
will hurtle down,
blue as the cord that bound her,
once, to her own lost mother,
its fringes brushing his boots.
Up he'll clamber, hungrily,
ferret-quick, toward the song
he's heard—*Go dig my grave,*
both long and deep,
lay a marble stone
at my head and feet—
his body on the sill
blotting out entirely
any world outside the trembling
garden of her body
she's about to step beyond.

Rapunzel's Clock

Of all the gifts he could have brought her
that she would seem to have no use for
in the tower—a lawnmower, badminton set,
high-heeled shoes—
this clock was most whimsical
and harmless at first, a toy house
carved with vines, flaunting a frozen bird
that popped in and out, and was always
whisked away at the last chime,
back through clenched doors,
as though to store up the intervening hour
in undistracted darkness.
After a night of counting every hour,
they destroyed the clock's music
to keep it secret from the Crone,
though at night, while he slept,
she could still hear its lurching gears,
the tongue-less bird shuttling its muted cuckoos
inside the cupboard where she kept it hidden.
It became the tight heart
she tuned her body to—
the crumbs of afternoons, his absences,
the gaining dark. Blood days.
Days of waiting. Nights of visitation
and violent blooming.
So that in time she grew to need
the clock's white noise
beneath her own body's story—
its given loneliness, its brief,
incredible eruptions of hope.

Rapunzel's Escape

First *he* plotted it—
a ladder perhaps—
but where could we build
or hide it? Or a posse
of kinsmen, foot-to-shoulder,
to hoist me down—
but I objected. Too risky.
Too cumbersome.
Too many hands.

I worried.
And then *I* thought of it,
watching sister Spider contriving
a house in air: a skein of silk
to make a braided stair.
At last, a way
to allay my waiting,
turned these days
from aching desire
to new wondering: where
did he spend his days?
who touched his hand?
fed his lips?

He brought me rope
and I started it,
my left hand making a kind of loom
to loop and stitch the rungs.
I knew this was the right course—
to leave my mother.
I was starved for horizon.

I stitched. I thrived.
And while I worked
even my hair grew fatter.

All day, the black ice
of streams groaned and broke.

How transparent the exchange,
but I didn't see it then.
I was weaving new hair
to replace my own,
that must be shorn in punishment
and ransom. It was my old story:
the world for my body,
my body for the world.

Rapunzel Shorn

I'm redeemed, head light
as seed mote, as a fasting
girl's among these thorns, lips
and fingers bloody with fruit.
Years I dreamed of this:
the green, laughing arms
of old trees extended over me,
my shadow lost among theirs.
Where is my severed ladder,
the empty tower of my hair?
Let the birds fall in love
with it, carry it away.
Here on earth the river
is in love with itself.
To get there, I'll shove
sharp stones into my shoes
as the saints did, lest
I forget what it means
to walk again upon it.

Rapunzel's Braid

Long after it lost its girl,
the wind kept heaving its gifts
of fragrance and leaves
and gritty drifts of snow into the tower;
the tower itself roared like an empty shell.
The birds she'd tamed returned
and returned to the sill, the room,
picking each abandoned thing
to palest hull and meal.
At first, the severed braid
writhed on the cold flags.
Like all dying things, it burned
as fiercely as possible
for attention among the torn leaves,
the rain pooled on the floor
in mirrors of the sky's taunting anarchy.
By the time the mice and squirrels and birds
began to pull it apart, its burnished river
had faded into dull snakeskin,
a slipped noose. Still, for years afterwards,
it sought her out, strands helplessly
carried into the uplifted arms
and empty trunks of trees, into nests,
into pastures studded with animal droppings,
its song as thin as a line of ink,
its penned name fading, fading, then gone.

THE WHITE ROAD

Insomnia

If you pretend you are not alone,
or that you are well-born
and protected, then of course
you can go out and stand in the yard.
As you would do anything
you wanted to do.
But if you go out
like an adolescent in a car
on a back road,
like a suspicious farmer,
then you will feel the dark enter you.
Whatever roams the air tonight
comes anyway,
as your willful body rumbles on,
digesting and breathing
in spite of your rigid watchfulness.
Let the footfall outside the bedroom window
be your own.
Take the white road that burns
past what endures but cannot move.

Paradise

And will there be a last man,
standing in palindromic irony
at the broken wall of the garden,
all his children long gone, and his woman
conceding one last thing—
the borrowed rib slipping out into red dust—
before she lies down in it, herself again,
turning back into merely *woe*?
And all the beasts of the field
and fowl of the air, having given back
the names they never wanted,
not caring enough even to trade them
among themselves, make the air thick
with animal noise—
Does it scare him, at the last,
how little life belongs to language?
Even the face of his own dog
is gibberish, snuffling among the fallen stones.
Inside, it's all still there,
the lapsed context—
all he needs to do to return is to stop
calling for help, is to drop to his knees,
nostrils awakened, bawling, saliva spooling down,
and crawl back over, the way he would have left
in the first place,
if he had really known anything.

A Doubt

It's nothing, a mordent
of the spirit,
a small fall
like the exhalation
of a breath;
the way that,
for just a moment
after the ribcage sinks
in a house
where someone is dying,
there is a silence
so deep, it is impossible
to tell its source
or to believe
the beating,
a small, sharp scruple
in your own breast.

McCoy's Hands at the Piano

The left's a preposition and its noun,
laid out and down, built up and knocked over.
The right's a verb, both active
and being, a tight warped knot
that the fingers ravel and unravel.

Sometimes the left is a large tree trunk
with its elastic wind-tossed basket
of branches, and right is the birds
alighting there, weaving wreaths
and nests, then springing out in long, wild scales.
Or the right is leaves emerging,
sharp and real—leaves soughing
and singing, tearing away and screaming,
then stirring again, like a promise
in the left hand's shimmering glove of ice.

Think about the bird's body,
most whole when most apart
and extended over the invisible.
How its body abandons itself
to fall from air to earth,
collapsing above the branch, then
miraculously erect and perfectly formed
among the leaves of the tree,
whose limbs have ridden death a hundred times
to witness such transformations.

GLASS TOWN

1. E. Brontë: Last Hours

In one vertiginous moment,
she knew that her bones
and all the convoluted circuitry
that sat upon their throne
had turned to water.
Panting in the back passage,
her wrists sunk in an apron full
of raw meat joints,
even the dogs' anxious snuffling
at her skirts must now be held
in light esteem, her art
of starvation almost a moot point—
that rapture of weightless violence,
the inner work that had sustained her
when the "world was lost" to her,
but wasn't, really. Not yet.
Each tongue, each tooth of language
had held her here until this moment.

2. "Buried Alive"
   C. Brontë: Twilight

The house ticks with migrainous music—
on the landing, her father's clock taps
against its cabinet, its grimly rocking pendulums
mocking the opened front gate, the smocking
of Queen Anne's Lace and feverfew tangled there.
She's looking out through the taunting arbor
and beyond, across the broken orchard of headstones
in the churchyard, to the pocked wall of the tower,
into which her father has discharged his angry pistol
each dawn for twenty years.
This is the hour she should belong
to nothing, not the dark eyes
of potatoes she's flicked out
with Tabby's knife,
not the stoveblacking, not the lapful
of needlework: whipstitch, and blanket,
and chain. And not yet to the lines of black ink
she'll cast herself into later, Papa in bed at last—
still all inward darkness, I left
. . . about twilight . . . Is she thinking
of him, then, of her *master*, her Belgian *monsieur*,
the dank smoke of his cigar
among the espaliered quince of the parterre—
each scribbled admonishment in the margins
of her old school essays still a thrilling
garnish of hope? The wirey, faded copses
and brambles of his scrawled, off-hand remarks
she studies, throwing herself against them
repeatedly each day—in the absence
of real letters—though outside
birds throttle the dusk with song,
and her *sorrow touches none with pain,*

and, beyond her, through the steeply pitched,
shabby houses of the villagers, infested
and overworked, the cobbled road
passes, whiter as the dark descends.

3. C. Brontë at the Sea
    Burlington, 1838

Here, I'd hoped to feel
unpunishable and free—
my knotted self flung open
across an escapade so endless
even *my* eyes couldn't hold it—.

But now I see that even the sea
is governable, its relentless,
bidden cresting and tumbling,
its sigh of hurtled secrets.
Here, silence is turned to **tsk** and tears,

inside out and raw with depths.
No bather, I watch others
wade the sandflats, slick
with mystery, their naked, unsuitable feet
assaulted by the husk-strewn surf

and the terrible powers.
I watch—my lot—caught
in its invisible, cosmic staves,
vainly deciphering the semen spray,
the diminishing stone.

4. Writing *Jane Eyre*
    Manchester, August 1846

Lover, crawl back to me
through these thorns,
a briery hedge of words erupting
in these rented rooms of enforced shadows
and silence, where my father lies,
felled and sleeping, his head swathed in bandages—
the ripe films that blinded his eyes
having been excised, and replaced with healing's
own dark dressing. The street outside
is somnolent with pavement
and dull, mechanical noise, and dusty,
shadeless trees. In here, the nurse
comes and goes, her basin wound with cloth
and witchhazel. I've ordered the meals,
mutton and tea. And, when I was asked
to do so, I was witness to the operation,
my father's eyes pried open, two murky orbs
that the knife's blade circled and unclouded.
My tooth aches, irksome reminder
of me. But see how far I've brought her,
my Jane? She has *as much soul as you—*
and full as much heart. Do you think
that your *stained truth* can go unpunished
in such tales? Go ahead, write
a shoemaker's address in the margin of my letter
before you tear it up. I'll have you.
But not before you wrestle through this barbed
kingdom of my making, and it thieves
those kindled eyes that measured me
by *mortal flesh* alone, and not before
you climb, fumbling your way along the walls
by touch, to this hot attic, arrested
in a feverish spell, where, my love,
I have not been sleeping.

5.   T'Parson's Anne
          — "Anne's nothing, absolutely nothing."
          C. Brontë, *My Angria and the Angrians*

This morning she would have me tear
the clothes from the bed we share, gasping
"the snow, the snow, I cannot bear
its weight," and, sure, her fingers gripping mine

seared, all chilblains, fever, ice.
Eager always to be going forward, away,
what pelting December storm was she mining,
dogged by duty, our mild disdain, and the barking,

tubercular cough that Ellen, who is with us,
ministers to with Gobbold's and carbonate of iron?
We are here at No. 2 Cliff, and outside
it's still May, Scarborough, the bay guiltless

as a glass of water. Yesterday, she would ride
upon the stony strand in a donkey cart,
all gray bird bones in a quilted pile,
nearly invisible but for the driver's tender fist

of a face and our own stricken masks,
walking beside her. Still, I tell you,
if one of us was born to bear the weighted task
of a man above, beside, beneath her,

it's this girl, our "dear little Anne,"
whose motion outshines my ire, and Emily's
paralyzing instinct, and Branwell's quick capitulation—
nearly all of us, now, shamed by Death.

Out of Haworth she took herself, and throve
a while without us, and out she would be carried
one last time, in Papa's arms, to the carriage that strove
to bear her here. And out of bed she rises now,

and will not let me fasten her waist
or move the chamber pot from beneath the bed.
She sits at the window by the sea, place
of the little lie she allowed herself,

drawing small, decided breaths
faithful as the waves below,
their small shoulders hunched,
an obliterating blizzard of flux and light.

6. Glass Town: A Childhood

Day sifted slowly, like sand, filled, and then tapered off
to an early, pointed stillness.
Always, the glass funnel of orphaned hours
hung, an empty womb above us—.

Night fed us—first with the haunted noise
of our mother's absent, asthmatic laboring,
silenced now, across the yard, beneath the heavy flags
of St. Michael's and All Angels.

We grew into this darkness,
clutching one another in bed, our hearts
skipping under a snow of covers that the oblivious
moon lit, and crossed, and then abandoned.

We built—in our cramped, stark room—a kingdom
of asiatic fronds, and heaped-high banquets, and grand,
prismatic, hyperbolic vistas, peopled by heroes and heroines
we'd mate and slay and *make alive* again.

The glass towers of our *verdopolis* rose like stacked, transparent
threadspools, the hordes we'd amassed clamoring
with anger, with *ire*, with their own dramatic hungers—
and still we persisted, desperate genii, stoking, accruing,

racing against the gaining morning
and its dismal call to waken;
we climbed all night, as though we might reach again
that infinitesimal aperture, abstract and far-off as heaven,

that once flooded open, implausibly, to bring us here.

Piano

for Donald Justice

Red quince branch,
curved and oriental,
drops blossoms
on the black shoulders of a piano.
Black ship, burial box:
inside, slaves chained together
shift their bracelets and moan;
the felted hammers wait
asleep as weights in a clock.

At the end of a long hallway,
steps.
Hands rise from a lap.
Light strikes the face of the sleeper.

String Quartet

Festung Concert, Salzburg

Then they were seized,
the four bodies,
the burning staves.
Seized ourselves,
we did not think of them
beyond this picture.
Instead, the skeins of hair and catgut
and the cries of wooden instruments
transported us from that castle room,
whose window ledges were so wide
a person might easily lie down
and watch the green Salzach coursing
between the fortressed monastery
and the domes and tiles of the Alte Stadt
that, from this dizzy height,
like the Mozart,
seemed all spires,
cream and light.
Even the air
seemed something we could ride.

After that concert on the mountain,
we made our way down with the others
in a thrall of silence,
as though the music continued
constructing itself,
teasing us out of time
as it carried us through it.
Little flashlights sketched the road.
Later, while we slept,
still buoyed by music,
in another country
some swell of sky, or sea,

or spirit tossed your father's body
gently from his bed.
He lay there, curled on the carpet
as if asleep, while we lay together
in bed, a place we'd taught ourselves
as children
not to fall from, even in dream.

Inside me our son swam,
sculpting the lake
in his waxy sheen of vernix,
the pads of his fingers
already wrinkled
with the whorls of self.
When storm clouds piled
and flickered with charges of light,
how strange the swollen windowcurtain
seemed to us, in bed, coming toward us
like something invisible thrashing
in a bandage,
a figment so odd
in its contorted familiarity,
that we sighed when it lifted,
and the wind and rain blew coolly in—

February 29

Above the kitchen table where my children color,
their big calendar frames a drawing—
blue African elephant, endangered species,
in whose large mother belly
floats a baby elephant,
fully formed and smiling,
a red valentine
pulsing in its center.
Below is the usual grid of numbers,
including this one, leap day,
taunt to time,
reminder that physics
makes its own music.

Twenty years ago, another February—
I was walking to school
after months spent trying to starve myself
back to a self before self-consciousness
and the heavy confusions.
Fourteen years old,
all seventy pounds of me trekked
the stretch of ice and mud
behind our neighborhood.
At a corner of the brick building,
wind tore me
for a split second
from the ground.
A specter at the lockers,
butt of jokes, snickers,
horrified stares,
I turned the dial, studied my combination,
the way I was still trying to figure out
how to be me in a body
with its own insistencies.
Outside, on the way home,

I felt something
in the restive hedges, their stark
gray lines turning into something new,
like my pencil drawings,
stacks of them: young women
with thickets of hair,
full, soft breasts, complex faces.
Their rooted legs held gowns blown
by bracing but benevolent winds.

Today, at the kitchen table,
my 4-year-old turns from the picture
she's drawing—Rapunzel
with a bristling kingdom of hair,
bows, legs that curve up—no problem—
in a "J" where the page bottom happens
to end too soon.
And now she spins out
into the room, dancing, grabbing underpants
from the laundry basket for a crown,
her own live hair spouting out
through the leg holes.
Though she sings and twirls to the taped music
from a kids' pop movie—
"I want much more
than this provincial life!"—
I know she's still happy in her world,
in her body, flying
by her own volition,
defying the motion of time
or any other power that takes away
instead of giving back.

Love Poem

> Why was I born
> if it wasn't forever?
>   —Ionesco

I want to give you
more than these words
finite as husks
or a string of barbed wire.
I want you to see
the blue knot my fist made
cast down against this page
in sunlight so bright
it seemed to swallow
the marks I made here.
How the chuckling shadows
of full-leafed trees
swarmed around me while I wrote,
as though winter
were some remote, impossible joke:
and how they lengthened eventually,
like the day,
into roads straight as rods,
slabs of gold, consoling sun
on either side
denying that there ever really are
any other paths
than the one we finally take.
I want to give you
what you cannot see here,
the shadow of my body
spilling across your face
when you lie under me,
as deep and intangible
as honeysuckle or any living thing
that heaps its fragrant weight
against a fence,
trusting it, forever.

Finishing *Jane Eyre* on the Grounds
of the University of Pennsylvania Hospital

"Reader, I married him"—or so Jane said,
and so I read. *Untrue* was how
this last chapter struck me as I began it,
apocryphal in its happiness

as the white ghosts who moved among us
on noiseless shoes of health, as the criss-
cross of November boughs above
that mocked us as we walked the grounds,

patients cagey in our incendiary
zones, past the sunken pan-pipes
of the laundry's smokestacks,
the barred wards, a family of metal deer

beside the public drive, impaled like cutlery
on the leaf-strewn lawn—and beyond our fences,
rows of mendicant brownstones
and metal-latticed shops beneath a *fuck*-scribbled

platform from which we felt the acrid shiver,
the hellish clank and roar of the el. . . .
I carried her here, my Jane, in a still-
unpacked suitcase—Jane, pale root

in the blue corridors of the dormitory,
smallest Jane starving in the fire's outer circle.
Jane beneath the wild plums, the bitter, floral
star of his cigar smoke in her mouth,

disbelieving it, seeing only
the necessity of loss—*"like the necessity
of death,"* but exploding nonetheless: *"I have
as much soul as you—and full as much heart!"*

—and for months, my not eating,
refusing the gym-class, the metal locker
of adolescence, seducing hunger, fucking
thirst, afraid to swallow even my own

saliva, leaving it in pools on the school
linoleum, behind the pew at church, giving
it all back—breasts, eggs, *elán*
vital—an insensate **no.**

Still, I was afraid for **her** to end, my Jane!
And so I slow-pedalled, closed the book
I'd started back in the English class
of my former life, got up and walked

the grounds again, circling, circling,
this time over to the ribs of fence, beyond which,
beneath stripped elms, double-dutching girls
my age saw something—me?—screamed, and fled;

and then the tall, impassive patient
with crossed arms I often passed as I walked
stepped up behind me, saying "You are nothing
but a setting sun," before moving on.

On better days, I wished to be a simple
chair, to hold without feeling.
"Reader, I married him" seemed a phrase
too full, too forgiving for the stark

sentence I was translating, the collapsed
vowels of self, the rickety scaffold of body
caught, like the trees, in a sleight
of sight, all the more *marked*

in a blaze of disappearing,
a death-wish to *be seen*—
I wanted that distinction. Still,
somehow, I unpacked my clothes,

and, one afternoon, backbone to a tree,
read the last chapter through.
It was not so much the marriage,
the baby's black eyes,

Mr. R's miraculous recovery
of sight that troubled me, but Jane's mention
of St. John, her pious, unsuccessful ex-suitor—
why end the book with *him*, why make *his* words

the novel's last—full of a missionary's
self-less zeal for death, his certain reward?
After all, angry Jane was who I longed to be, hurling
a book, missile-shot to the head of a cruel

boor, strange Jane, singing her orphaned
changes over my shoulder, hymns of ransomed
ire, wings of plainness, wings of desire—
Why, then, after risking—and winning—so much,

why end the book with *St. John*,
Arctic loner, exiled by faith?
On a chaperoned outing to the Museum of Art,
I stepped down, buoyed by the plush,

concert-hush of hoarding,
into the catacomb of an Egyptian tomb,
past the gilt carapace of mummies and walls
adorned with men and women contorted in impossible

postures, rendering every part
of the body visible at once so that no stray
appendage, no plate of figs, might be left behind
in the transport to the next life—

and I thought of blue Jane, breaking ice off the basin,
refusing the mirror. Jane gnawing on a stone.
Jane's stricken fugue across the heath,
begging among bees. Jane at the window of health.

Was Jane my angel, then?
Even now, I read but balk to end
her tale, put it down ten times
before I circle around to the last passage

that disturbs me—why?—for its turn
away from love's knit thrall, its redemptive
net—until I remember—it *was* St. John!—who,
practicing duty, lifted Jane, thieved and dying,

from the threshold where she lay, inadmissible,
unadmitted. He *saw* her. And so he haunted her
ever after, implausible and real.
Like my hulking fellow patient,

the stranger who stalked the paths
with me and Jane back in those lost days,
who swerved one day, tilted toward me, seizing
my hands in his huge paws, surprisingly girlish

and soft: "My god," he cried aloud—
an odd, high-pitched child's voice—
"they're the claws of an old woman!"
so that everything in me rose, at last, to defy it.

April

Bridal skirts of weeping cherry,
jilted by recent rain,
and the chimerical plum along the median strip

are washed with pinkish
hallucinatory white, and a slick
oceanic light suggests everything:

the signs, the fickle, strobing traffic lamps
reflected in the street, the whoosh and wake of passing cars.
Wet birds that blow apart the lawns

with sudden rising. On such a day,
I feel forgiven, as though I had new need
to be, as though winter were a blame

I carried in me always,
dragged along the ground in babyhood,
lugged higher as I grew, a glacial fist

clenching and unclenching inside
its neighborhood of bone and gristle.
The loopy signature of telephone wires

transmits inaudibly above; clouds break open.
Fresh draperies of pollen. My tires grip the gravel drive
that popples like another shore

and, turning the wheel, I find
I'm home, my armpits darkly sweet
with this sudden thaw that floods

my throat, my palms,
my nose, my eyes with helpless,
senseless absolution.

Biographical Note

Lisa Russ Spaar was born in Elizabeth, New Jersey. She teaches poetry writing at the University of Virginia, where she also administers the MFA Program in Creative Writing. The author of two chapbooks of poems, *Cellar* (Alderman Press) and *Blind Boy on Skates* (Trilobite/ University of North Texas Press), her work has also appeared in *Poetry*, *The Virginia Quarterly Review*, *The Kenyon Review*, *Ploughshares*, *Shenandoah* and elsewhere. She is the editor of *Acquainted with the Night: Insomnia Poems*, published by Columbia University Press in October 1999. She lives in Charlottesville, Virginia, with her husband and three children.